Vintage Maps Central Park and New York City

All rights reserved. This book, or parts thereof, may not be reproduced in any form without permission. Images found in this book may have been retouched.

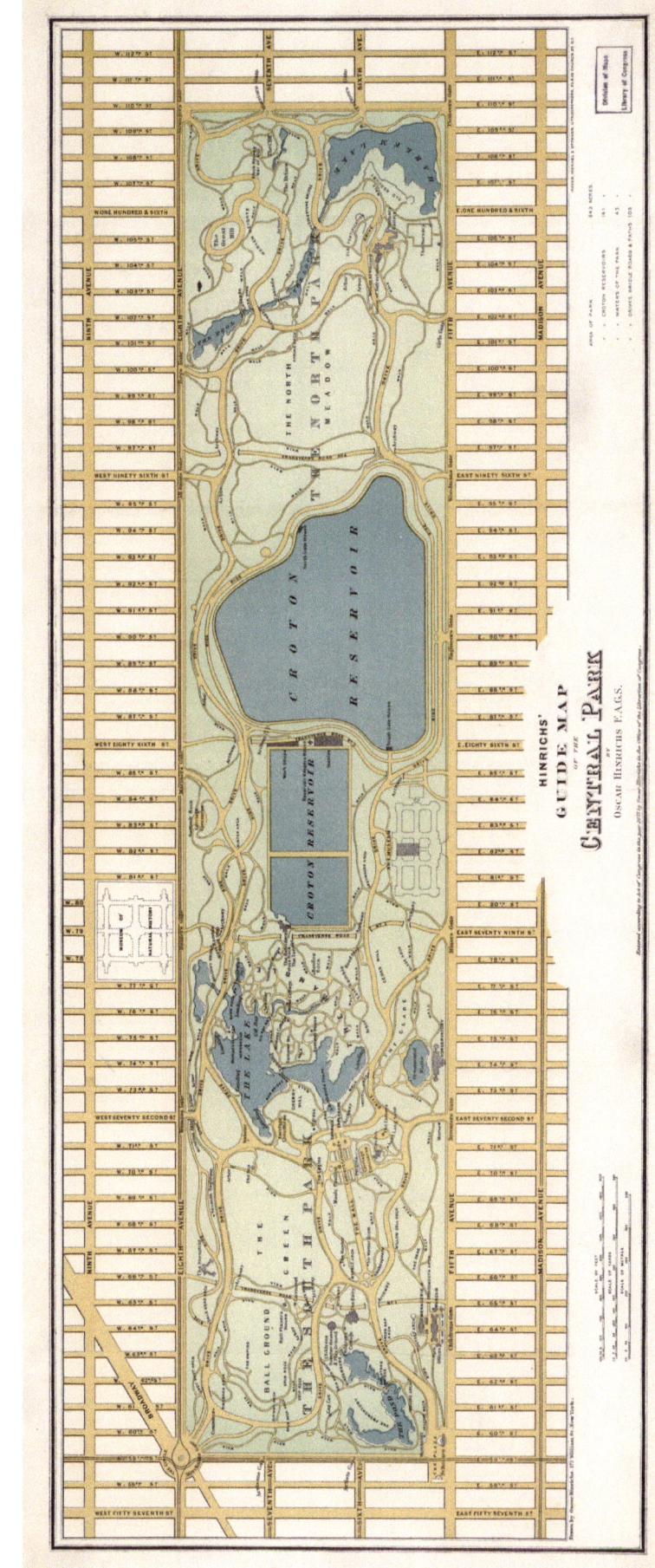

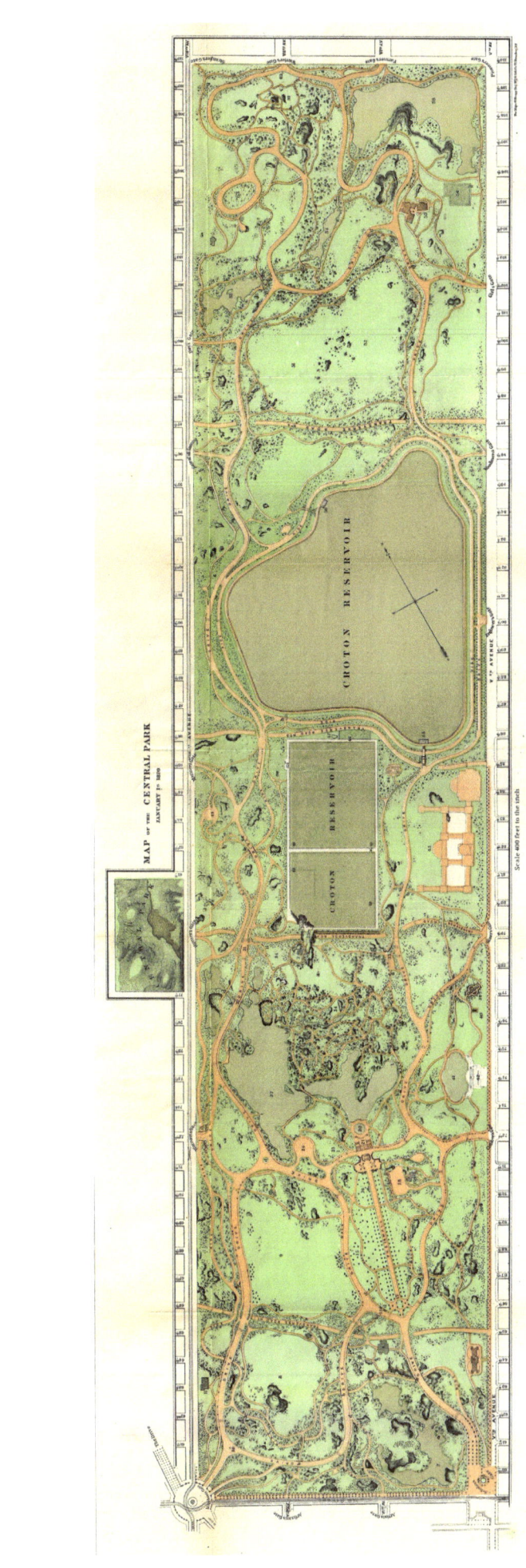

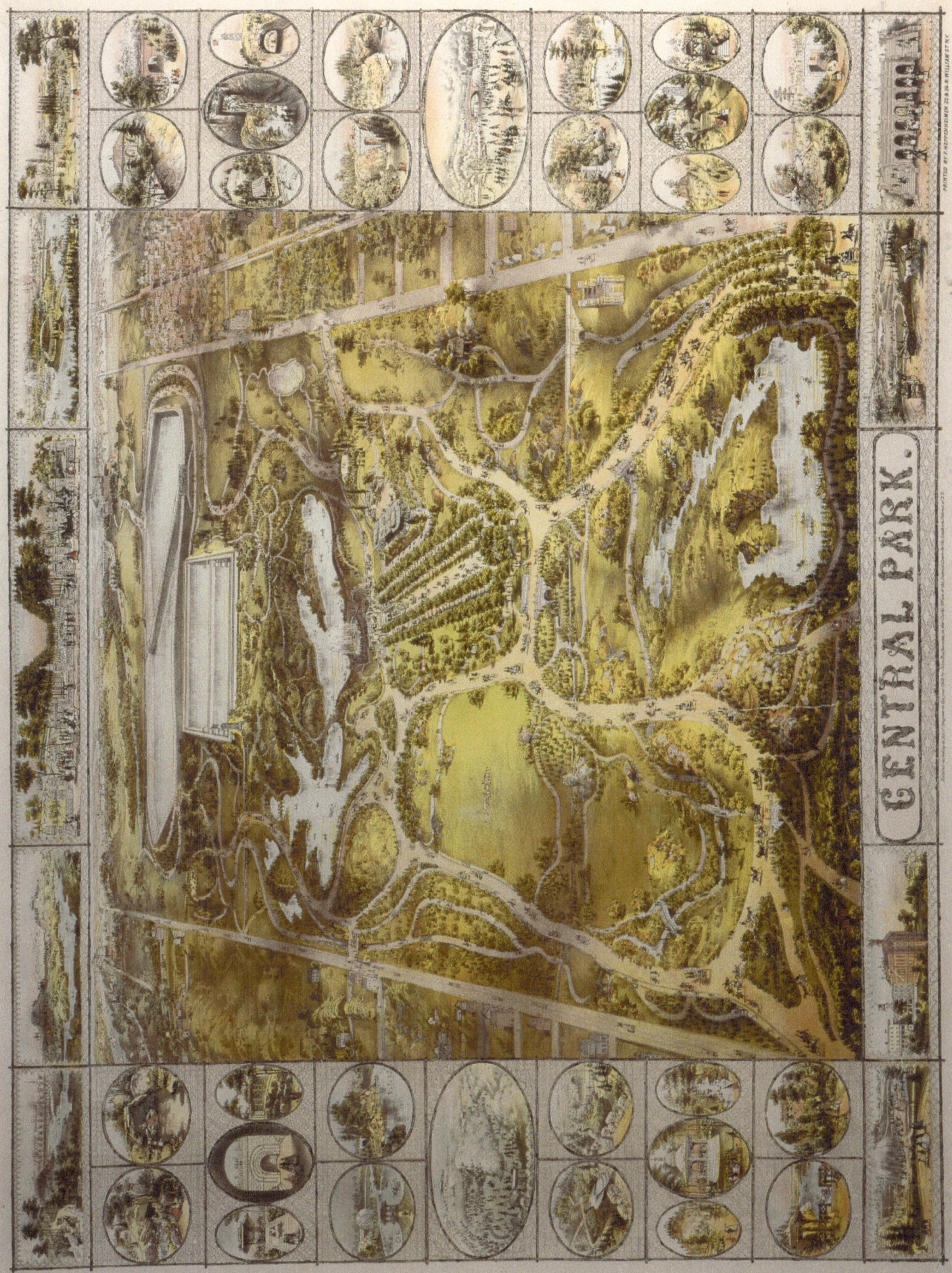

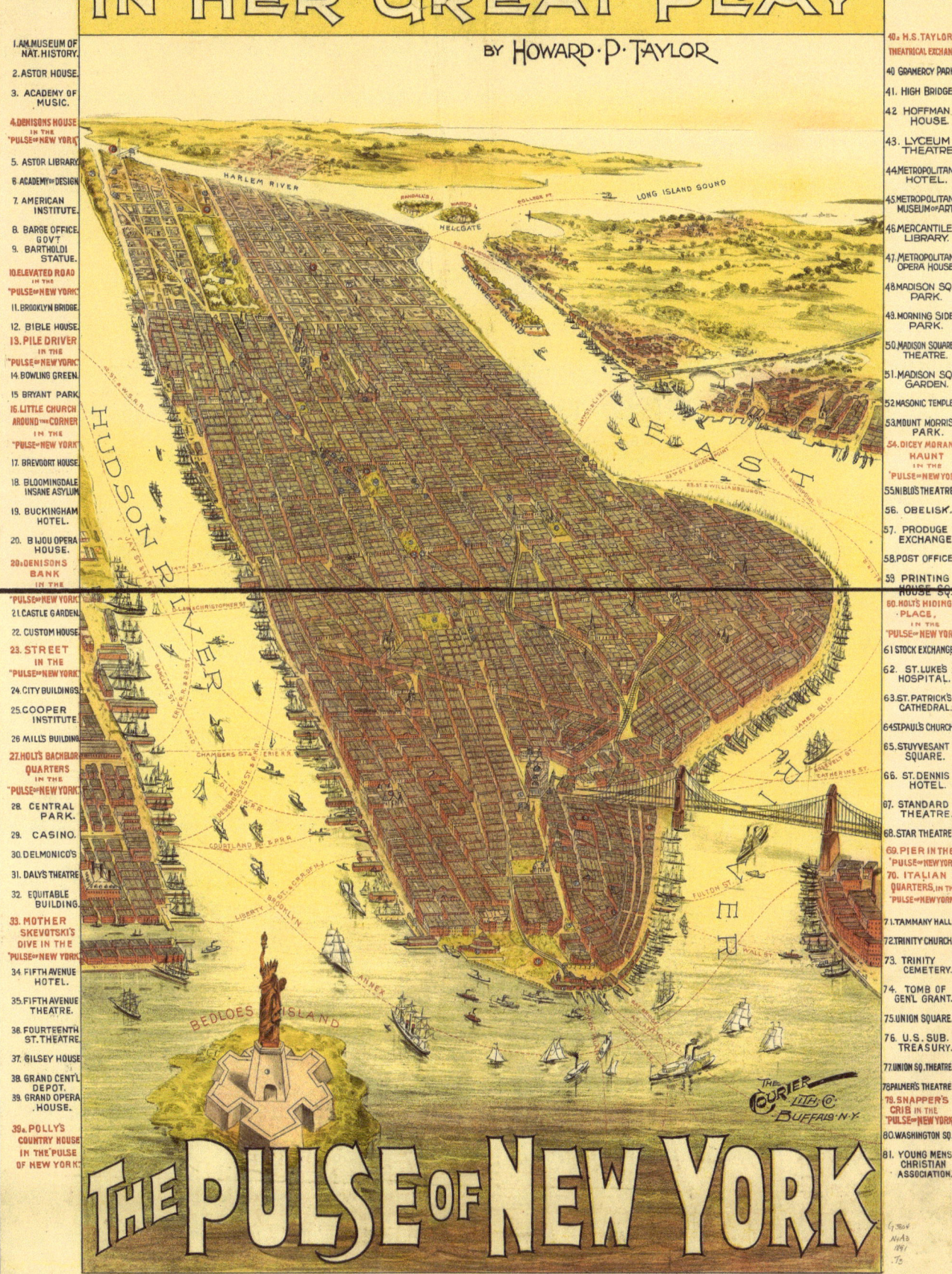

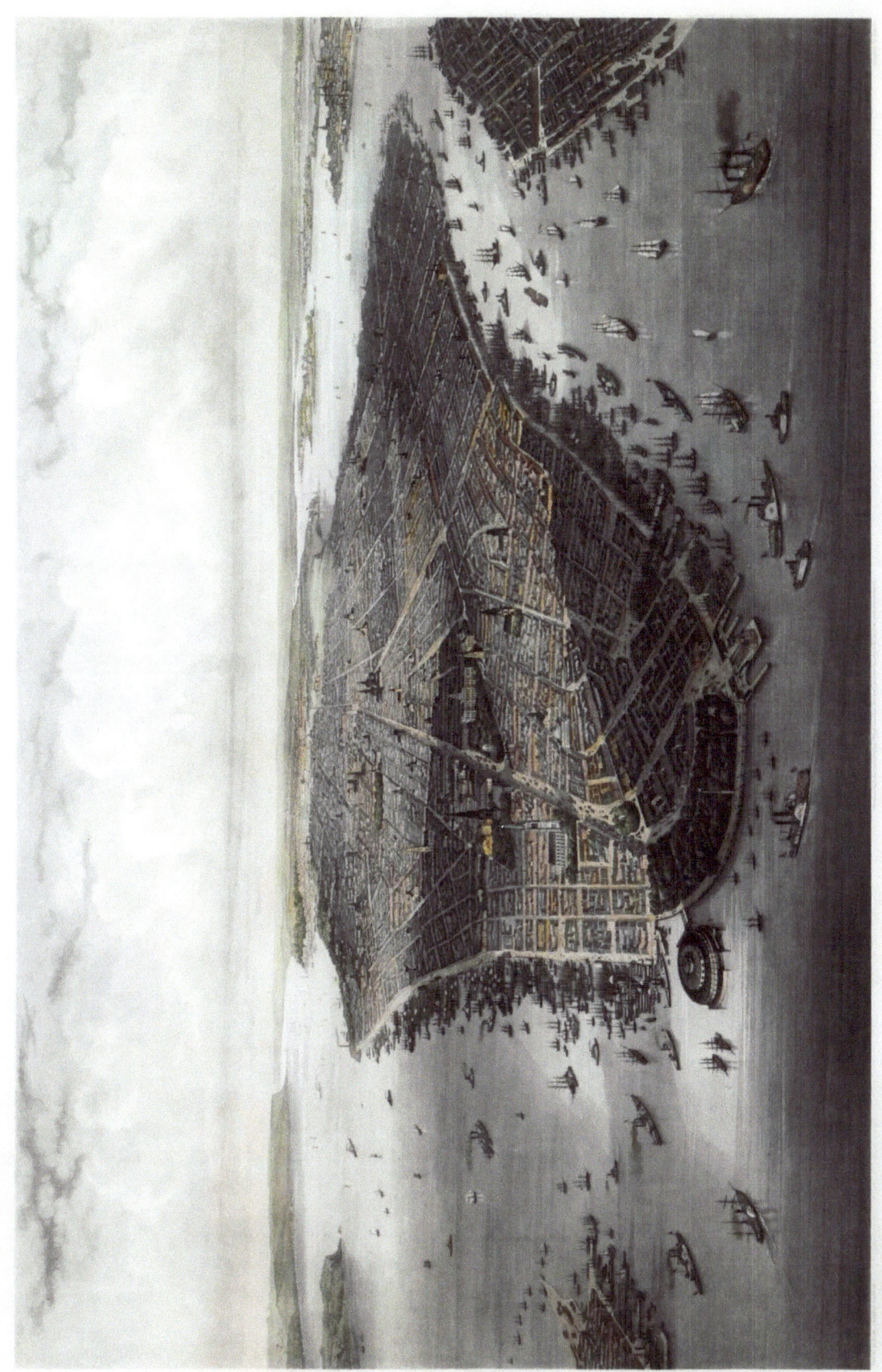

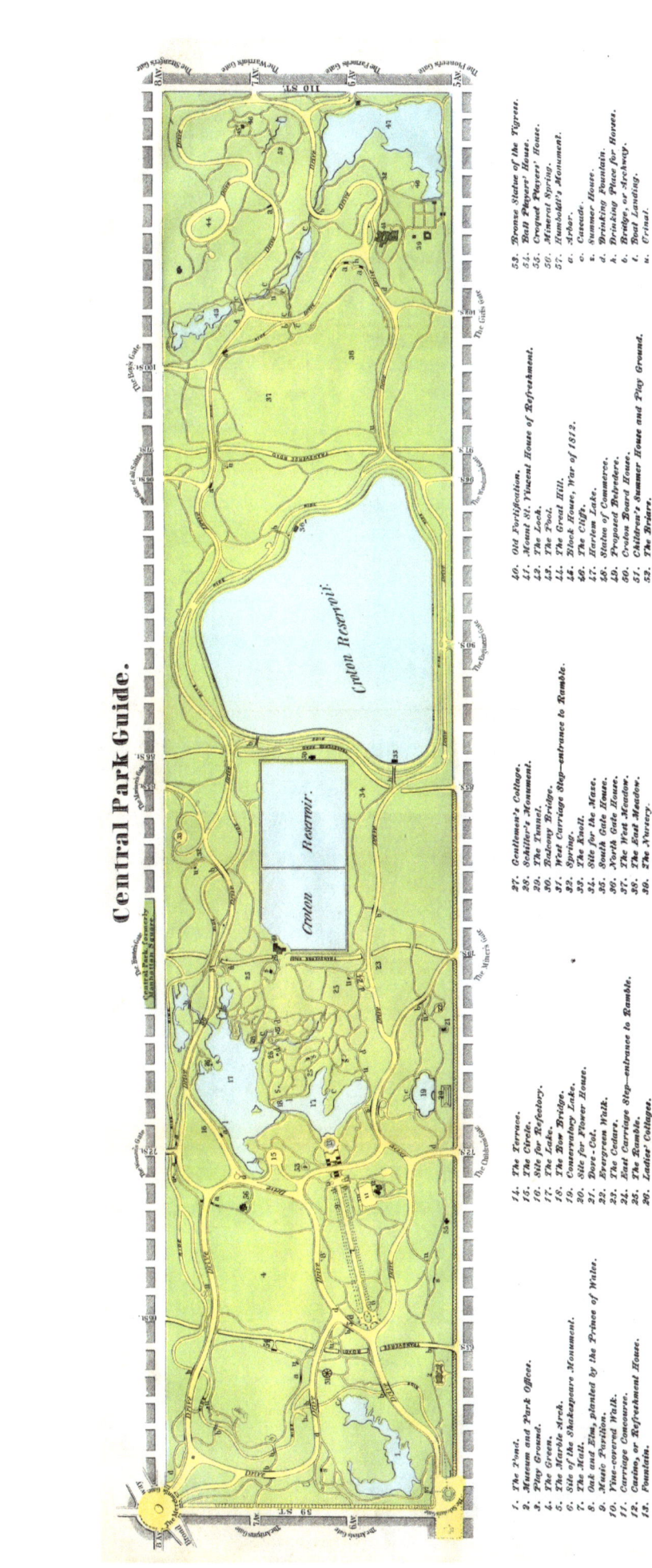

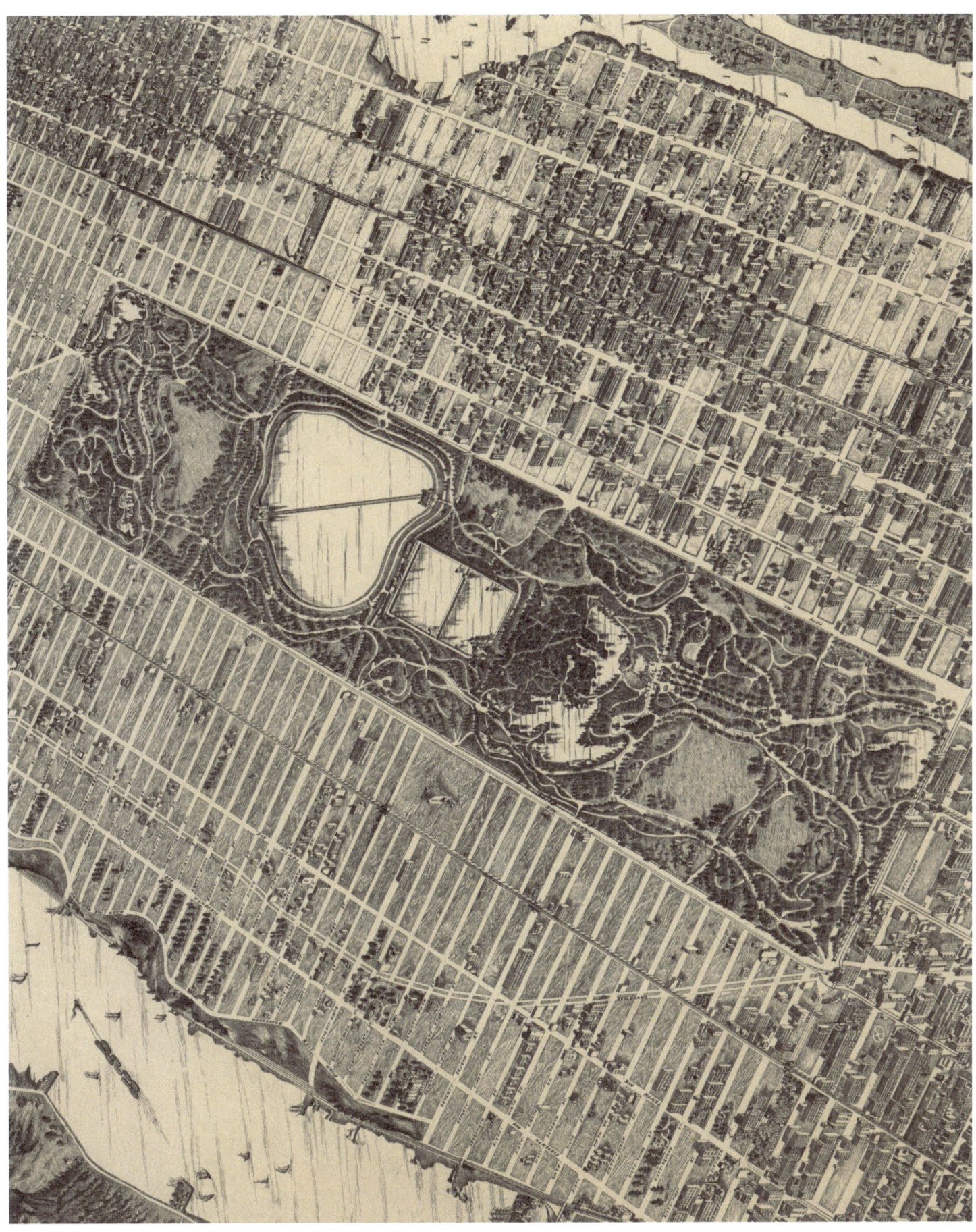

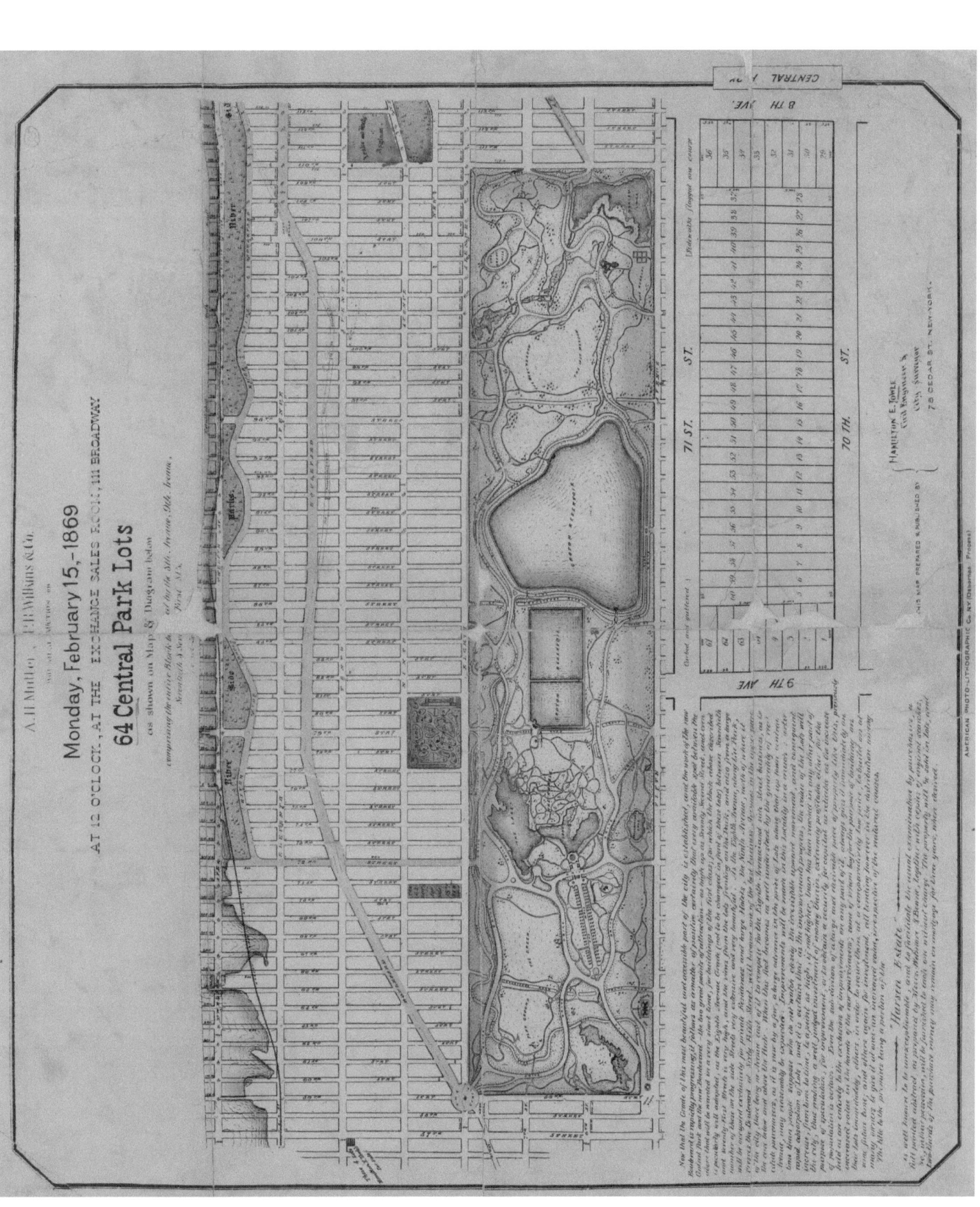

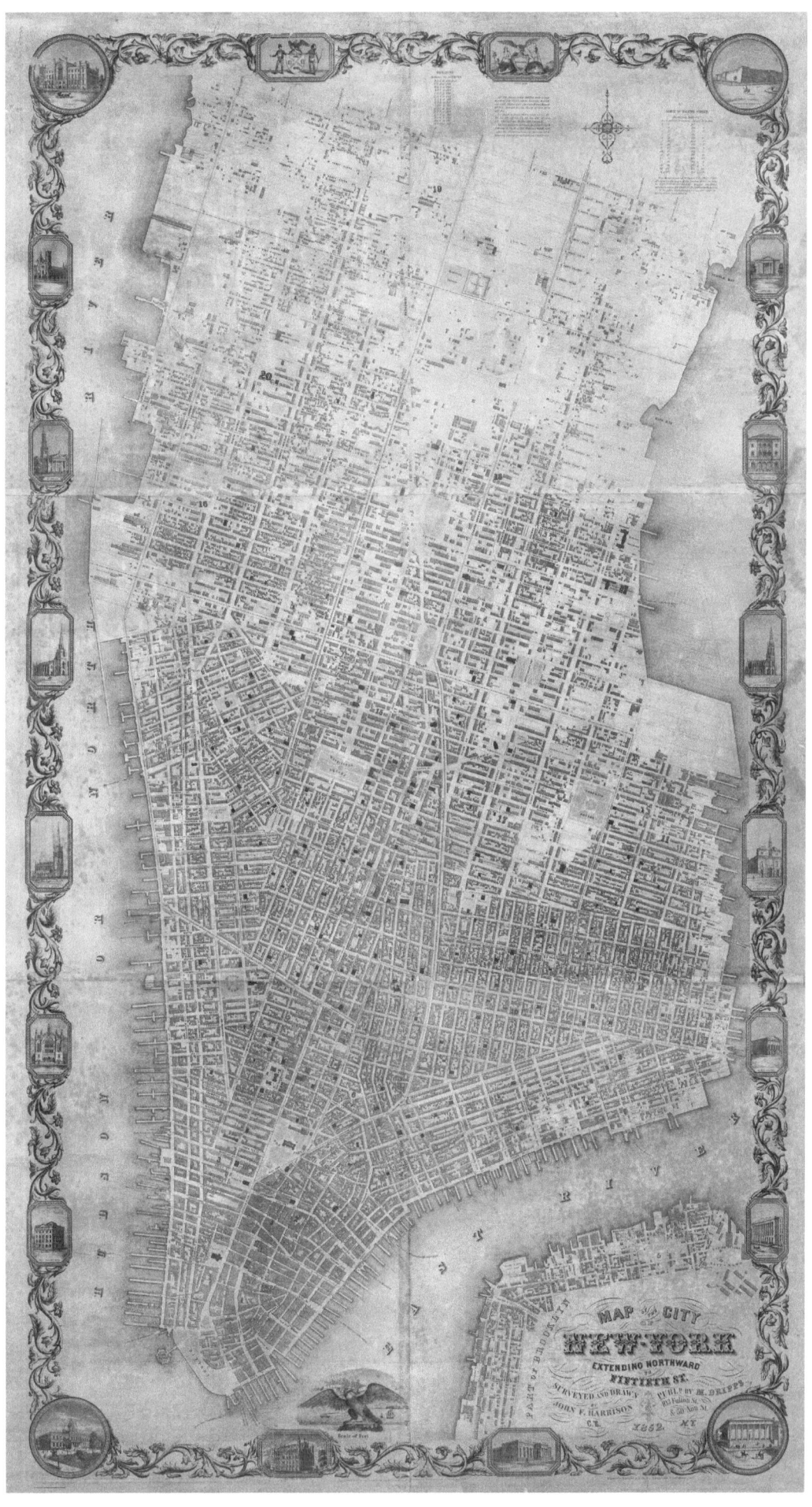

COLUMBIA GLACIER,—ALASKA'S TYPICAL ICE TONGUE

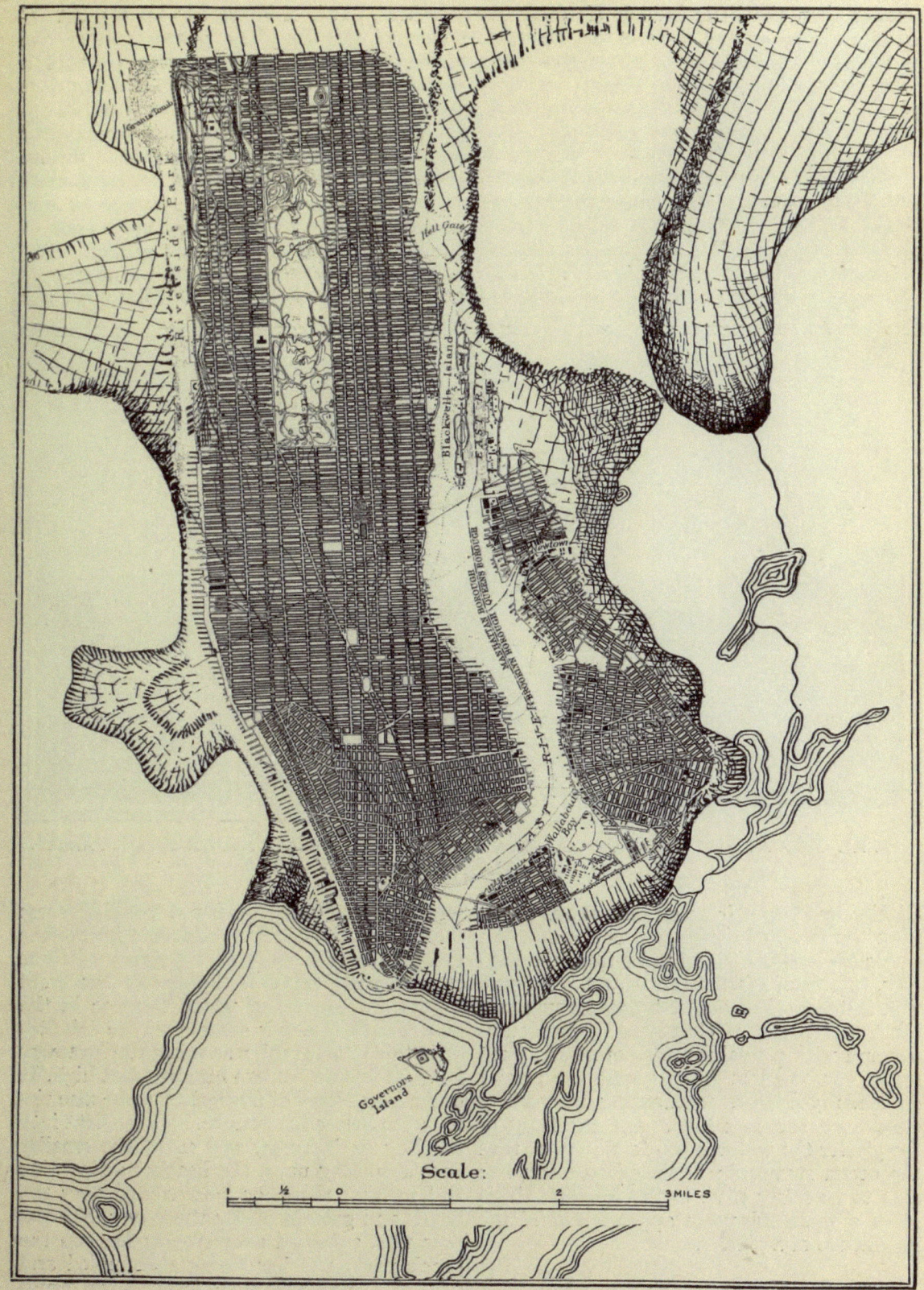

MAP OF THE BOROUGHS OF MANHATTAN AND BROOKLYN, NEW YORK CITY, SUPERIMPOSED ON THE LOWER PORTION OF COLUMBIA GLACIER

(The Battery at the terminus of the glacier, with Brooklyn Navy Yard near the eastern and Hoboken and Jersey City near the western margin)

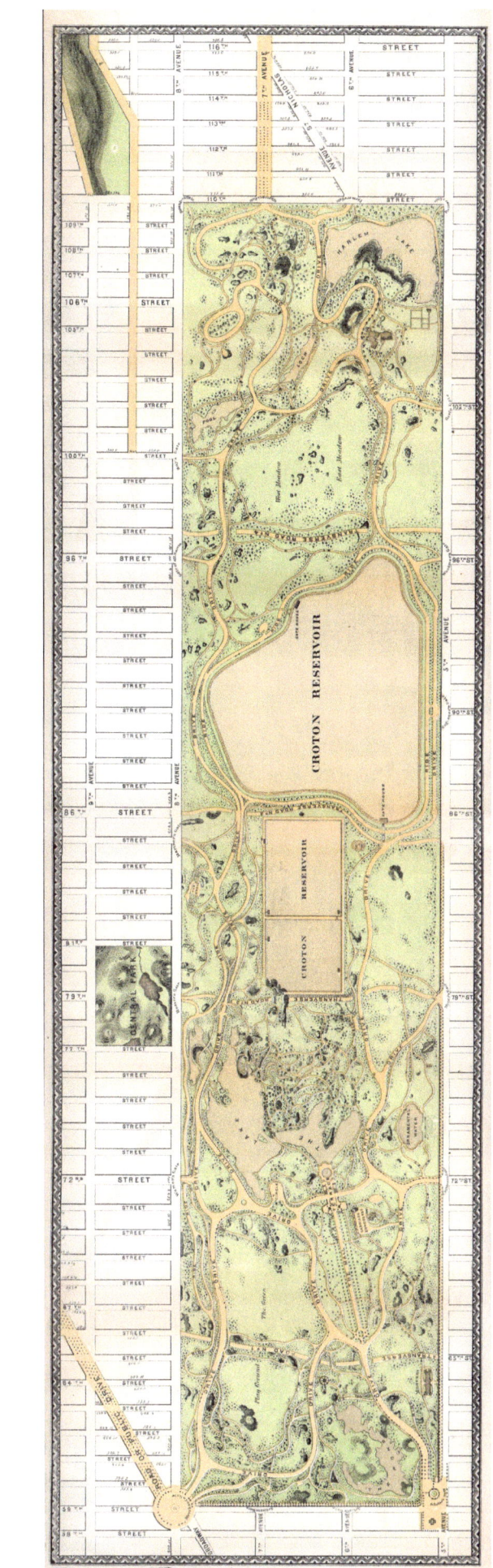

PLAN OF THE PARK.

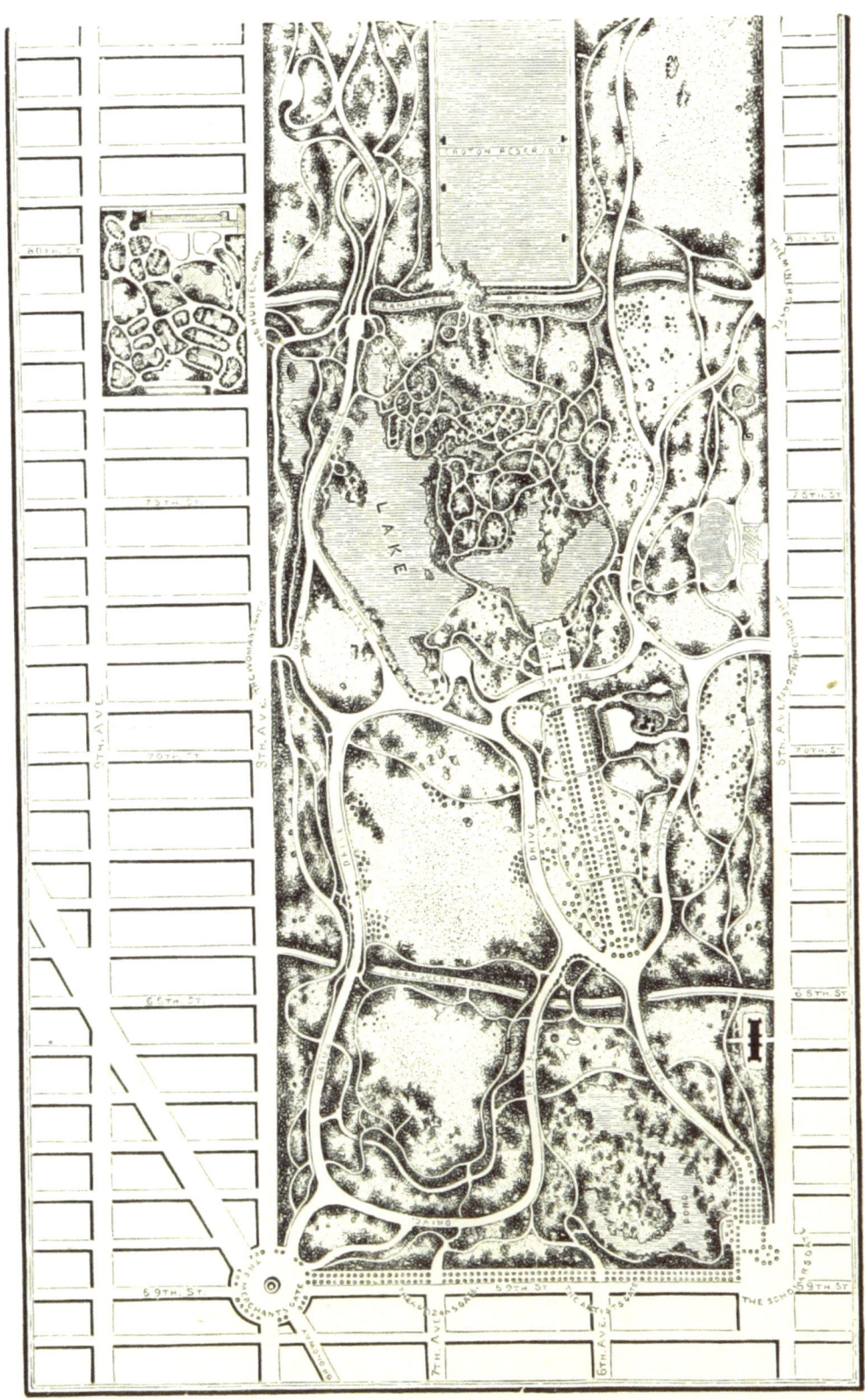

THE SOUTH END.

THE NORTH END

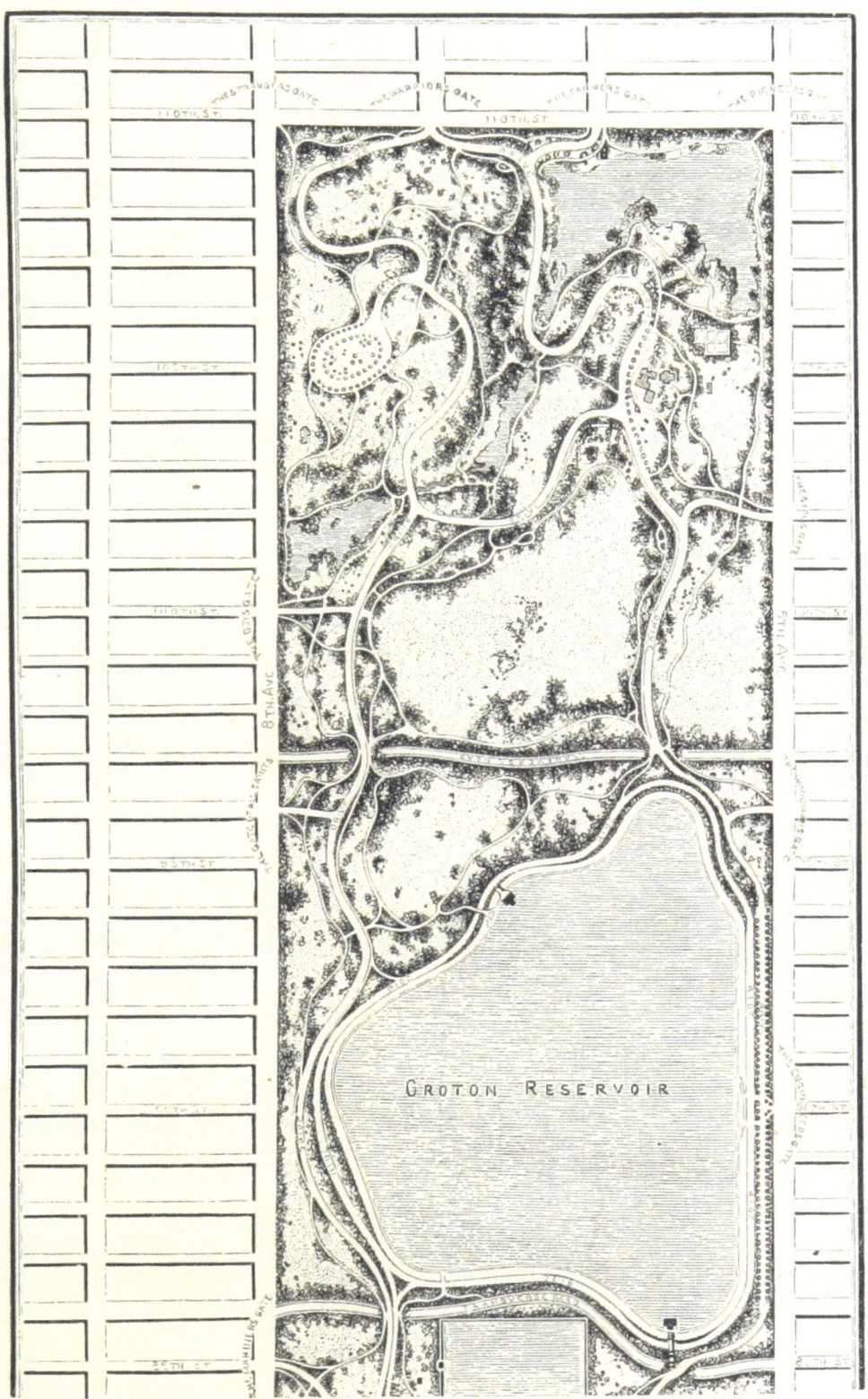

PLAN OF THE PARK.

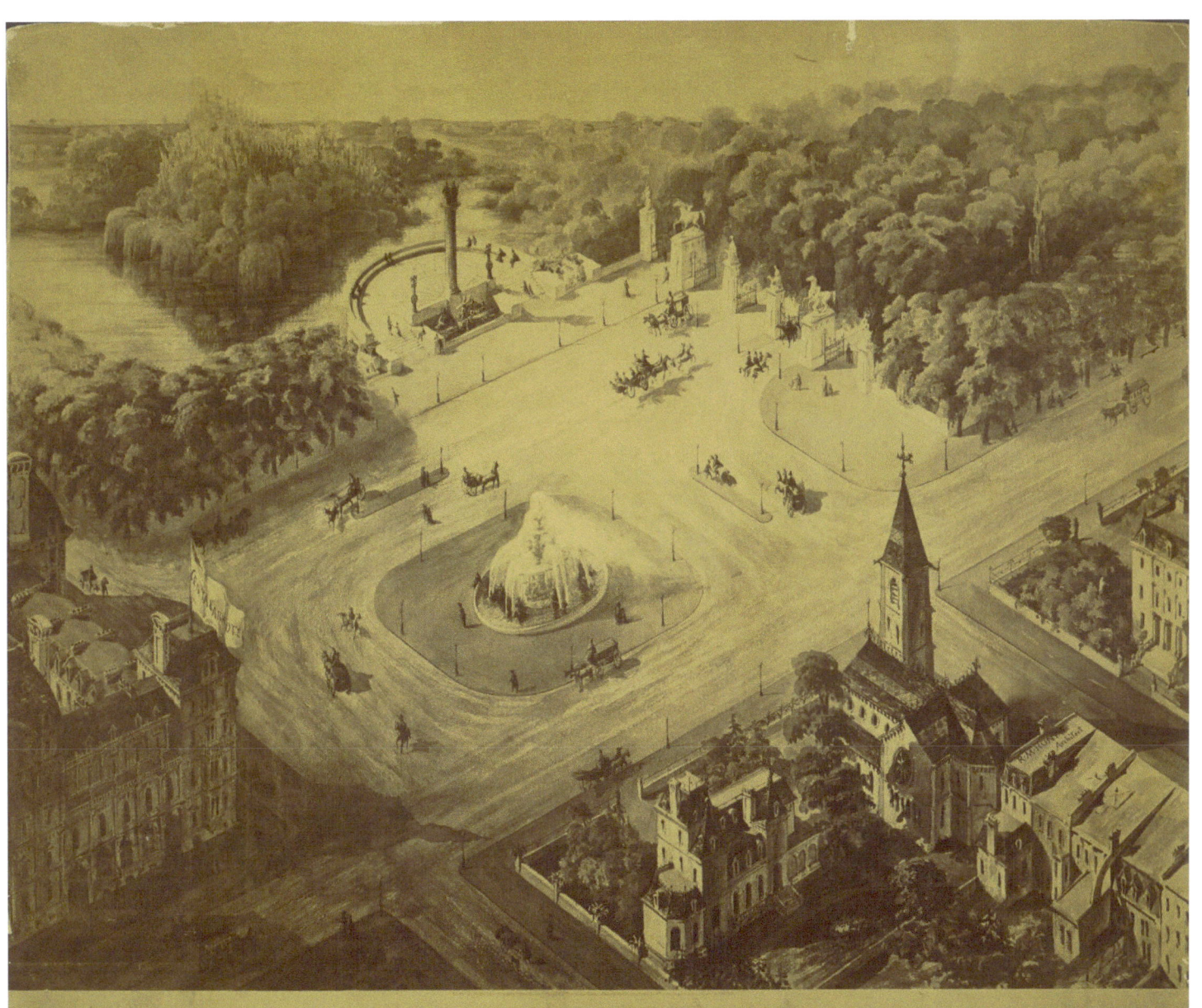

CENTRAL PARK
ENTRANCE AT CORNER OF FIFTH AVENUE AND FIFTY NINTH STREET, DESIGNED BY RICHARD M. HUNT, ARCHITECT, AND ADOPTED BY THE BOARD OF COMMISSIONERS OF THE CENTRAL PARK.

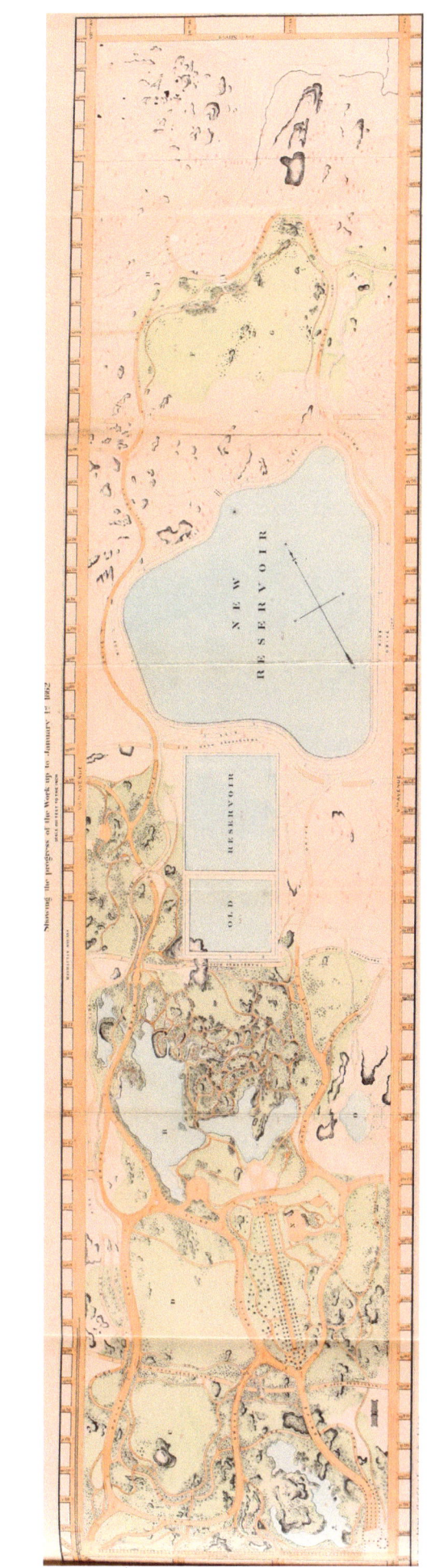

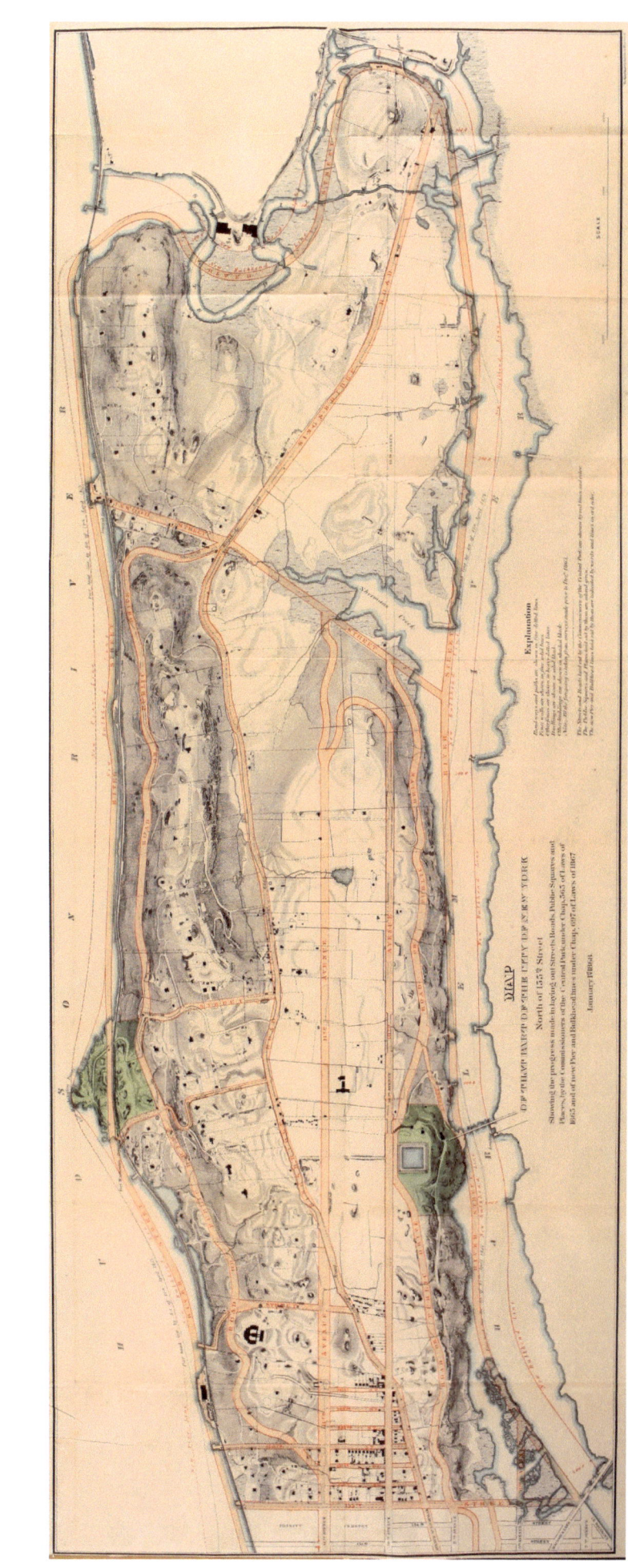

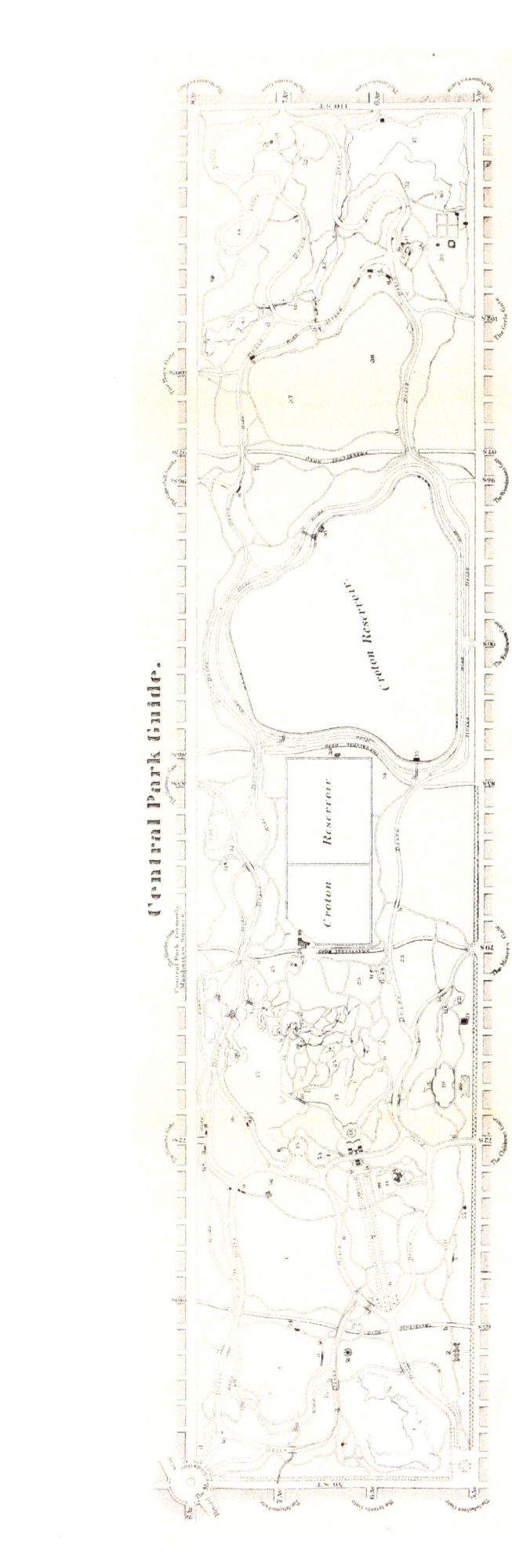

Südseite von New-York und Brooklyn mit der projektirten Kettenbrücke. (S. 8.)

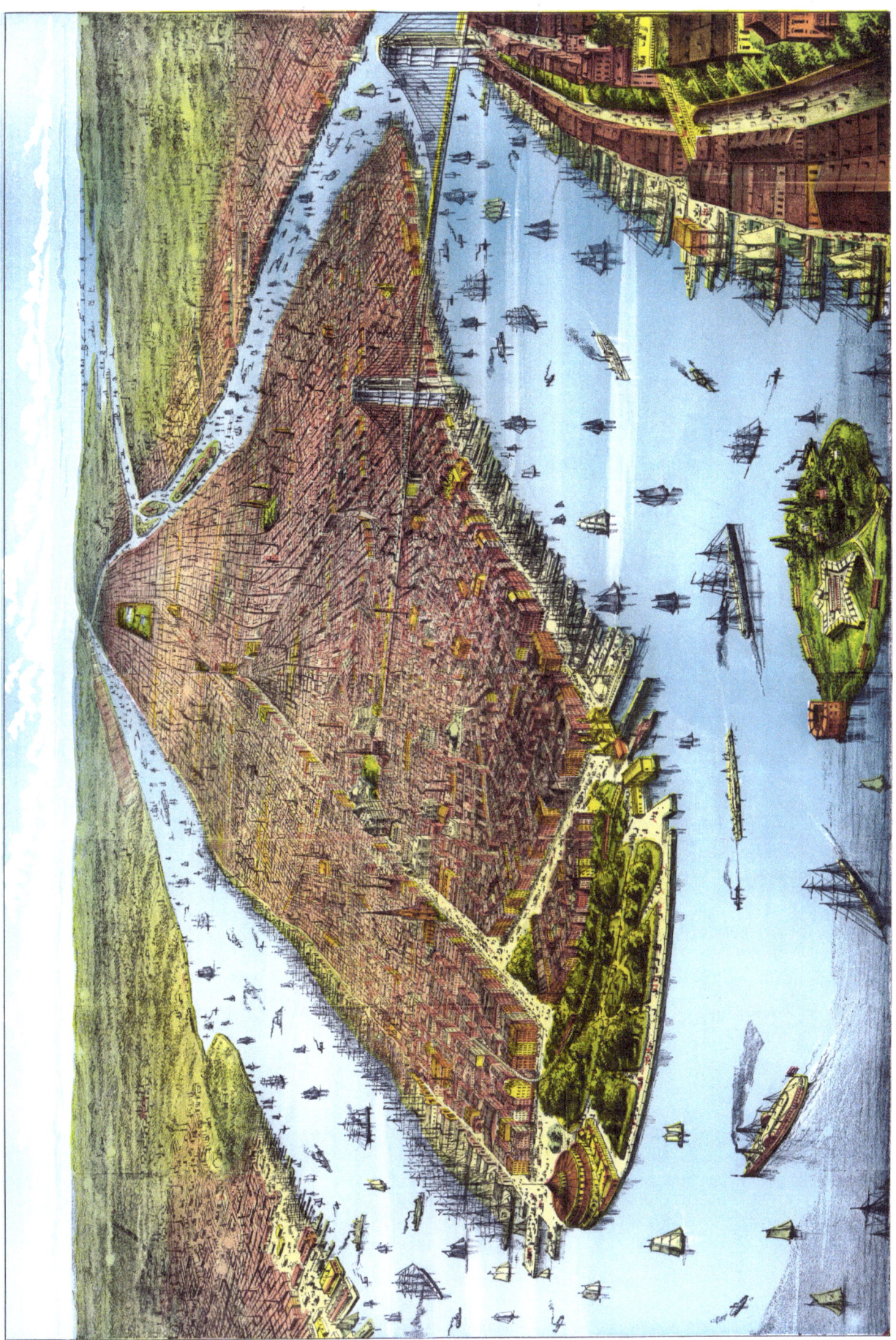

NEW YORK.
FROM THE HARBOR.

COPYRIGHT, 1879.

THE CITY OF NEW YORK — SHOWING THE BUILDING OF
THE EQUITABLE LIFE ASSURANCE SOCIETY OF THE UNITED STATES.